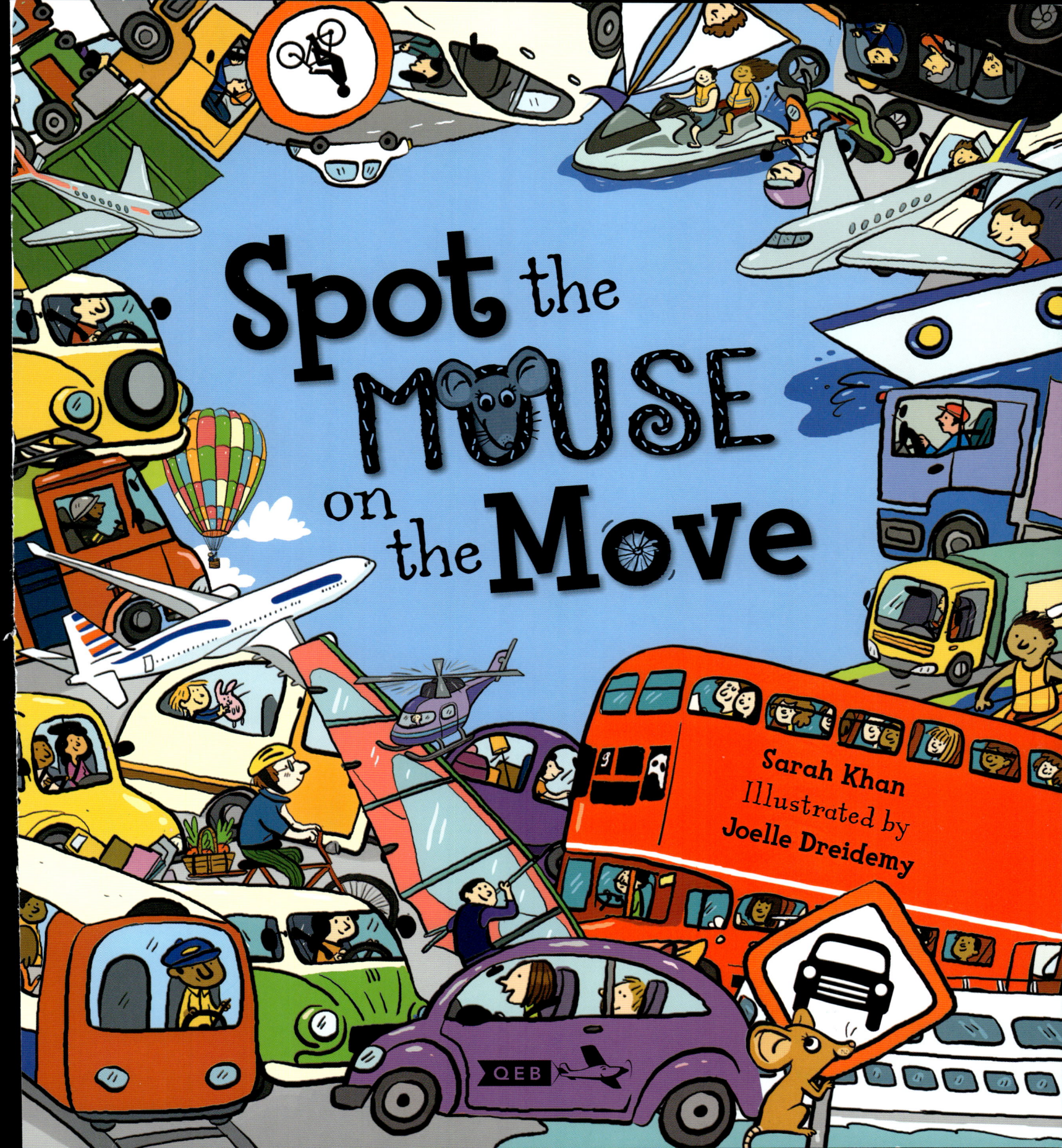

The MS Ulysses is one of the world's largest ferries. It has 12 decks and can carry 1500 vehicles.

You can find all sorts of tents and trailers at a campground. Big ones and small ones—all built for fun!

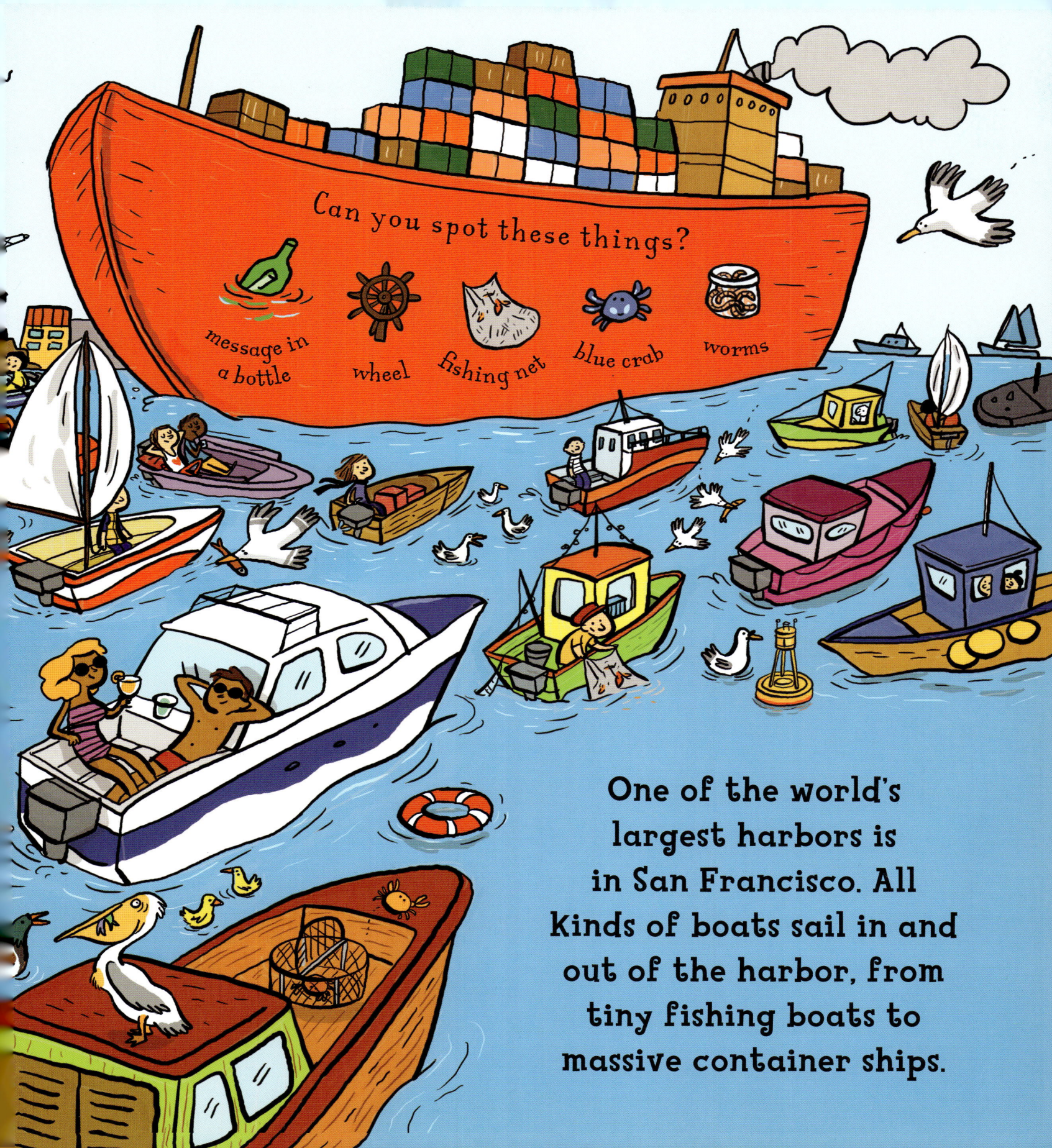

More to spot

Go back and find these scenes in the book!

Did you find me?

More fun on the move!

Sailing boat

Cut a triangle from stiff paper and make three holes down one side. Weave a drinking straw through the holes to make a sail. Stick modeling clay to the bottom of the straw then fix your sail onto the bottom of a plastic container. Now float your sailing boat on water!

Hide and seek

Choose a cuddly toy that you can hide around your home for a friend or family member to spot, just like the mouse in this book! You could hide other objects too and make a list of things to find.

Alphabet game

When you are on the move, look out for the letters of the alphabet on signs or car license plates. Can you find all the letters of the alphabet in order, from A to Z, before your journey ends?

Cardboard bus

Paint a cardboard box or cover it with colored paper. Paint or draw wheels and windows onto the sides. Cut out pictures of people's heads and shoulders from magazines and stick them onto the windows.

Publisher: Zeta Jones
Associate Publisher: Maxime Boucknooghe
Editorial Director: Victoria Garrard
Art Director: Laura Roberts-Jensen
Editors: Tasha Percy and Sophie Hallam
Design: Duck Egg Blue and Mike Henson

Copyright © QEB Publishing, Inc. 2016

First published in the United States by
QEB Publishing, Inc.
6 Orchard
Lake Forest, CA 92630

www.qed-publishing.co.uk

All rights reserved. No part of this publication may be reproduced, stored in a retrieval system, or transmitted in any form or by any means, electronic, mechanical, photocopying, recording, or otherwise, without the prior permission of the publisher, nor be otherwise circulated in any form of binding or cover other than that in which it is published and without a similar condition being imposed on the subsequent purchaser.

A CIP record for this book is available from the Library of Congress.

ISBN 978 1 60992 820 9

Printed in China